Welcome to

Tidings of Comfort and Joy

Carols provide more than just a soundtrack to the Christmas season. They lead us in worshipful responses to God's love made known and connect us to precious emotions, traditions and memories. They also tell the story of stories, helping God's truth linger in our minds and hearts. But they can also become so familiar that we stop really hearing their words or truly receiving the revelation and wonder they sing out. As these daily devotions revisit the poetry and meaning of some of your favourite carols, we pray they will bring you a fresh sense of the timeless wonder of the incarnation and the very present help Jesus is still bringing to the Middle East and its people today.

Each day's short reflection will:

- introduce a different carol
- offer thought-provoking reflections inspired by it
- share real-life stories of hope and transformation from Embrace's work
- lead you in prayer
- provide optional ideas for putting Christ's comfort and joy back at the centre of your Christmas celebrations.

Thank you for spending Advent with Embrace the Middle East.

Bethlehem carol sheet

Twenty-one of the most popular carols featured in Tidings of Comfort and Joy, together with more real life stories from Embrace's work in the Middle East, are available in our Bethlehem carol sheet.
Call **01227 811646** or visit **shop.embraceme.org** to order free copies for your church or community group, or to browse our other Christmas resources and products.

Bethlehem
carols
music CD

Bethlehem
carols
music book

Bethlehem
carols
unpacked
book

Contents:

Tidings of Comfort and Joy

God rest you merry, gentlemen

Pause and wait: for a few moments.

We are about to start retracing the steps of an old journey in new ways; to walk across holy ground in our hearts – and the Middle East – as we prepare the way for Christ to enter in more fully again. Are you ready?

Enjoy today's carol:

God rest you merry, gentlemen,
Let nothing you dismay,
For Jesus Christ our Saviour
Was born upon this day,
To save us all from Satan's power
When we were gone astray:
O, tidings of comfort and joy,
Comfort and joy,
O, tidings of comfort and joy.

At Bethlehem in Judah
The holy Babe was born;
They laid Him in a manger
On this most happy morn:
At which His mother Mary
Did neither fear nor scorn:
O, tidings of comfort and joy...

From God our heavenly Father
A holy angel came;
The shepherds saw the glory
And heard the voice proclaim
That Christ was born in Bethlehem
And Jesus is His name:
O, tidings of comfort and joy...

Fear not, then said the angel,
Let nothing cause you fright;
To you is born a Saviour
In David's town tonight,
To free all those who trust in Him
From Satan's power and might:
O, tidings of comfort and joy...

The shepherds at these tidings
Rejoiced in heart and mind,
And on the darkened hillside
They left their flocks behind,
And went to Bethlehem straightway
This holy Child to find:
O, tidings of comfort and joy...

And when to Bethlehem they came
Where Christ the Infant lay:
They found Him in a manger
Where oxen feed on hay,
And there beside her newborn Child
His mother knelt to pray:
O, tidings of comfort and joy...

Now to the Lord sing praises,
All people in this place!
With Christian love and fellowship
Each other now embrace,
And let this Christmas festival
All bitterness displace:
O, tidings of comfort and joy...

God rest you merry, gentlemen – Traditional English carol

Reflect:

The first line of *God rest you merry, gentlemen* is familiar enough that most of us can sing it without thinking. But what does it actually mean?

In the 15th century, when this carol originated, 'rest' had another sense. It was less to do with ceasing activity and more to do with remaining. Or, in this case, with God as the subject, being kept or held...

So we should probably be singing something more like *'God keep you merry, gentlemen'.*

Christ has been born! Nothing dark or unjust has the power to fully dismay us ever again – these are the tidings of comfort and joy so worth singing about – and so worth remaining in.

'For I am convinced that neither death, nor life, nor angels, nor rulers, nor things present, nor things to come, nor powers, nor height, nor depth, nor anything else in all creation, will be able to separate us from the love of God in Christ Jesus our Lord.' (Romans 8:38-39.)

As we enter Advent again 2,000 years after this news was first sung about in the Middle East, amid headlines that continue to shout about war and injustice in this region, we can still be confident in this same comfort and joy. We can remain steadfast in the knowledge of Christ's coming.

This isn't glib sentiment or stiff-upper-lip stoicism; as the carol freely admits – the world can, and does, frequently give cause for 'dismay'. But it rightfully sets this lesser reality in the larger truth of an abiding, determined and active hope; one that is born all over again every time we hear a new story of redemptive transformation brought about by love.

There are always tidings of comfort and joy... and we have many to share with you over the coming weeks.

Thank you for spending Advent with Embrace...

Pray:

Lord Jesus, bless me and keep me merry while I'm still waiting for all dismaying news to end forever. Help my heart to hear, and remain in, the very real comfort and joy the tidings about your birth still bring. And give me the faithful courage to remember and share your stories of transformation, so others can keep merry too.

Ideas for: remaining in comfort and joy

- 'Comfort' is not a particularly Christmassy word – but we need reassurance at Christmas just as much as at any other time. If you are finding the festive season difficult for any reason, you might find it helpful to read Isaiah 40, in which God looks forward to Jesus' coming by saying: *'Comfort, comfort, my people...'*

- Every time you see the word 'joy' this Christmas – on cards, decorations and even in advertising – let it spark a prayer for the Middle East. We're surrounded by so many negative images of the region – but by using 'joy' as a trigger-word for moments of prayer, we can remember and uphold all the positive work being done towards peace and justice.

Two pupils at Bethany Girls School, a school in the West Bank where local Muslim and Christian children learn together.

O Christmas tree!
O Christmas tree!

Pause and ask yourself:

what's your favourite Christmas tradition?

Enjoy today's carol:

O Christmas tree! O Christmas tree!
Thy leaves are so unchanging;
O Christmas tree! O Christmas tree!
Thy leaves are so unchanging;
Not only green when summer's here,
But also when 'tis cold and drear.
O Christmas tree! O Christmas tree!
Thy leaves are so unchanging!

O Christmas tree! O Christmas tree!
Much pleasure thou can'st give me;
O Christmas tree! O Christmas tree!
Much pleasure thou can'st give me;
How often has the Christmas tree
Afforded me the greatest glee!
O Christmas tree! O Christmas tree!
Much pleasure thou can'st give me.

O Christmas tree! O Christmas tree!
Thy candles shine so brightly!
O Christmas tree! O Christmas tree!
Thy candles shine so brightly!
From base to summit, gay and bright,
There's only splendour for the sight.
O Christmas tree! O Christmas tree!
Thy candles shine so brightly!

O Christmas tree! O Christmas tree!
How richly God has decked thee!
O Christmas tree! O Christmas tree!
How richly God has decked thee!
Thou bidst us true and faithful be,
And trust in God unchangingly.
O Christmas tree! O Christmas tree!
How richly God has decked thee!

O Christmas tree – Lyrics translated from the German O Tannenbaum, written by Ernst
Anschütz in 1824 after a traditional folk song.

A fair trade, hand-carved olive wood Christmas decoration made in Bethlehem.

Reflect:

Every year, around six million* living trees are consumed in the UK.

Almost every household has a Christmas tree of some type. But even among devoted Christians, very few people use it as a prompt for worship. Instead, it often ends up having more to do with the traditions that hide Jesus' presence, rather than those which reveal Him.

This makes a lot of sense. Evergreens in festivals around this time of year predate Christianity – they were used in both pagan 'Yule' and Roman 'Saturnalia' celebrations.

The Christmas tree itself came much later, but we don't need to know much history to work out that a fir tree is not central to the biblical account of Jesus' birth, or that it is more connected to the European landscape than the Middle East's.

O Christmas tree! O Christmas tree! was also 'borrowed' to provide a festive theological lesson. It started life as a secular folk song but someone spotted its potential and translated commonly experienced tradition into a unifying gateway to praise.

Jesus took this approach a lot too; the rich but familiar landscape, traditions and experiences of Jewish and Middle Eastern life were made into symbols for eternal truths. And His followers have been doing the same ever since…

***O Christmas tree! O Christmas tree!* illustrates that we too can revisit existing traditions, reshaping them so they point us towards – rather than away from – a joyful celebration of the One who is at the very heart of Christmas.**

---

* *Six million is the estimated annual figure for the number of Christmas trees bought in Great Britain cited by the British Christmas Tree Growers Association – www.bctga.co.uk – in 2016. Some sources, including The Guardian in 2014, also quote eight million as the total consumption number for the UK as a whole.*

Pray:

Lord Jesus, who opened Middle Eastern eyes to re-see bread, water, sheep, lilies and seed as symbols of a life lived for you and others, you have always led poets and saints to do the same wherever they looked ever since. Please open my eyes to see you more clearly too. Remake my Christmas tree, and all my other old traditions, rich with Christ-with-us meaning, and give me new ideas to awaken fresh wonder and renewed, faithful trust in you.

Ideas for: refreshing your traditions

- Egypt's Coptic Christians have distinct traditions of Advent and Christmas. During the Fast of the Nativity, they consume no food and drink between sunrise and sunset, and avoid animal products altogether. Could you take inspiration from them and simplify your life over the new few weeks, creating the space to see Jesus more clearly?

- When 'richly decking' your Christmas tree, you could do things a bit differently this year. Give each decoration its own special meaning, or give prominence to an object designed to prompt prayer for the Middle East. Embrace's catalogue features some beautiful decoration made in Bethlehem. Visit **shop.embraceme.org** to see the range.

The first Nowell

Pause and ask God:
to bring to life old words for a new context...

Enjoy today's carol:
The first Nowell the angel did say
Was to certain poor shepherds in fields where they lay;
In fields where they lay, keeping their sheep,
On a cold winter's night that was so deep.
Nowell, Nowell, Nowell, Nowell,
Born is the King of Israel!

They lookèd up and saw a star
Shining in the East, beyond them far;
And to the earth it gave great light,
And so it continued both day and night.
Nowell, Nowell...

And by the light of that same star,
Three Wise Men came from country far;
To seek for a King was their intent,
And to follow the star wherever it went.
Nowell, Nowell...

This star drew nigh to the North-West;
O'er Bethlehem it took its rest,
And there it did both stop and stay,
Right over the place where Jesus lay.
Nowell, Nowell...

Then entered in those Wise Men three,
Full reverently upon their knee,
And offered there in His presence
Their gold and myrrh and frankincense.
Nowell, Nowell...

Then let us all with one accord
Sing praises to our heavenly Lord,
Who hath made heaven and earth of naught,
And with His blood mankind hath bought.
Nowell, Nowell...

The first Nowell – Lyrics adapted from the Cornish original by Davies Gilbert and first published in Carols Ancient and Modern in 1823.

Reflect:

Reread the first two lines of the carol... they proclaim that the first ever Christmas carol was sung by angels.

But it was not sung in a religious space. It happened on an obscure hillside. And it was not sung to kings, politicians, businessmen, academics or priests – but to poor shepherds.

Although looking after sheep has been the work of ordinary people in most societies, shepherds in first century Israel were particularly looked down on by the rest of the community.

Jesus said He came to 'preach good news to the poor' (Luke 4, quoting Isaiah 61:2) and to 'seek and save those who are lost' (Luke 19:10); so this prioritising of the shepherds over other groups was entirely consistent with His mission and message.

This King of Israel was building a very different kind of kingdom – one where those on the outside would be sought out first.

It's worth pausing to think who today's 'shepherds' are; who are the outsiders looked down on in your community or in the various cultures of the Middle East today?

3 December is the International Day of Persons with Disabilities, promoted by the UN every year since 1992. The fact that the inaugural day is only a couple of decades ago shows just how recently the international community has realised that people living with disabilities need help in overcoming discrimination and exclusion, especially in poor communities.

It is particularly poignant today – in the context of our focus on carols – to remember people with hearing difficulties, who can be isolated from communication as well as opportunity.

Not six-year-old Amin though! Thanks to Embrace's partner, the Learning Centre for the Deaf in Beirut, Amin (a Syrian refugee in Lebanon) can now hear every piece of good news told to him through his new hearing aid; he's even been able to start school.

No more being left out for Amin. What joyful news!

Amin at the Learning Centre for the Deaf, Lebanon.

17

Pray:

Lord Jesus, let my life harmonise with the angel's first Nowell; help me to search out those who have been pushed outside, and make me ready to offer them my first and best. Please bless and resource the Learning Centre for the Deaf, Embrace and everyone who seeks to follow you in bringing good news to the poor, especially those celebrating and serving people living with disabilities across the Middle East.

Ideas for: blessing today's 'shepherds'

- Who are today's 'shepherds' in your own community and in the Middle East? Could you share with your church congregation, friends, or social media followers anything that has struck you about who society welcomes and who is left out in the cold?

- Alternative Christmas gifts not only raise awareness of issues but also make a practical difference at the same time. Our *Art therapy* Alternative Gift champions inclusion for people with disabilities. Giving an Alternative Gift is a lovely way to bring some of today's 'shepherds' into the heart of your celebrations. Browse our full selection of Alternative Gifts at **shop.embraceme.org** or in our print catalogue.

All with one accord

Communication is a vital part of human relationships, but deaf and hearing impaired people become isolated when others don't see them as part of the speaking and listening world. Supported by Embrace, the Learning Centre for the Deaf offers courses and DVDs in Lebanese Sign Language for all who want to learn – deaf people themselves, their friends and families, teachers and members of the wider community. This work of inclusion reminds society that everyone has something to say.

O little town of Bethlehem

Pause and ask yourself: what surroundings, circumstances or people help you feel at peace?

Enjoy today's carol:

O little town of Bethlehem,
How still we see thee lie!
Above thy deep and
  dreamless sleep
The silent stars go by.
Yet in thy dark streets shineth
The everlasting Light;
The hopes and fears of all the years
Are met in thee tonight.

O morning stars, together
Proclaim the holy birth,
And praises sing to God the King,
And peace to all on earth.
For Christ is born of Mary;
And, gathered all above,
While mortals sleep, the angels keep
Their watch of wondering love.

How silently, how silently,
The wondrous gift is given!
So God imparts to human hearts
The blessings of His heaven.
No ear may hear His coming;
But in this world of sin,
Where meek souls will receive
  Him, still
The dear Christ enters in.

O holy Child of Bethlehem,
Descend to us, we pray;
Cast out our sin, and enter in,
Be born in us today.
We hear the Christmas angels
The great glad tidings tell:
O come to us, abide with us,
Our Lord Emmanuel.

O little town of Bethlehem – Lyrics written by Phillips Brooks (1835–1893).

Reflect:

'Peace' and 'quiet' are two words that have become closely linked. But they are very different – and often don't belong together.

The biblical understanding of peace is 'shalom' – a rich, colourful sense of wholeness, rather than the absence of conflict or noise.

Quiet can often be a beautiful gateway into stillness and calm, but it can also be hostile, or signify emptiness, or an 'after-ness' that is anything but peaceful... The way a house sounds when a key member has left it forever; or a town centre feels when the businesses have failed; the way a disaster or bombsite sounds after the devastation has hit; or how a person might feel when they have experienced deep trauma.

There is a compelling beauty to the lyrics and melody of *O little town of Bethlehem,* which describe in word and mood a peaceful and quiet night when Jesus was born. But there is also some sentimentality at work here, which perhaps actually robs from the fuller life and colour involved with the reality of Jesus' birth.

It is much more likely that 'the wondrous gift' wasn't given 'silently', but with some considerable noise in the room where Mary was giving birth. But there certainly was peace – for Peace Himself was born that night in a town whose name will always be precious because of it.

Bethlehem today is in desperate need of 'shalom'. Some of its quiet is anything but peaceful, especially when it comes from traumatised children. One girl living in Bethlehem who knows all about painful silence is Rania. Until recently, she wasn't able to speak in school.

But comfort was coming because Rania was referred to the Embrace funded Bethlehem Arab Society for Rehabilitation, who work to support children in the community who have additional needs. Thanks to them, Rania's school began to understand her, allowing her to communicate in writing rather than putting her under pressure to speak. Now things are getting louder – because trust has been built up – and Rania is at peace enough to start speaking to her teacher.

Pray:

Lord Jesus, let peace be born again in Bethlehem today. Let it be heard loud and clear in the laughter of rehabilitated children, and in a new sense of expectant chatter among every age group of society as its people all hope, and work, for shalom. And if silence does fall – let it be a peaceful one.

A child at the Bethlehem Arab Society for Rehabilitation, a centre offering a wide range of medical care and rehabilitation support to people in the West Bank.

Ideas for: inspiring and blessing those who take practical action

- How much do your friends, colleagues and church members know about what the 'little town' of the Christmas carol is really like for children today? Talk to your church leaders about introducing a moment of silence at your carol service for the congregation to reflect on the challenges of life in modern Bethlehem.

- Perhaps, in the busyness of Advent's preparations, you crave some silence. Carve out some time to sit in a quiet place; use this time to remember that the child born in Bethlehem 2,000 years ago is already interceding for those who grow up there today. Join Him in prayer for them.

Hopes and fears

For more than 60 years, our famous Bethlehem Carol Sheet has created connections between UK congregations and the people of the Middle East. In modern Bethlehem, Embrace's partners face many fears and challenges – roadblocks, the separation barrier, a dwindling Christian presence and widespread poverty. Yet even in these difficult circumstances, their faith in Christ prevails, and the wondrous gift of new hope is born in them every day.

As with gladness men of old

Pause and think about: people – in the Bible, from history, or who you know personally – who inspire you.

Enjoy today's carol:

As with gladness men of old
Did the guiding star behold;
As with joy they hailed its light,
Leading onward, beaming bright,
So, most gracious God, may we
Evermore be led to Thee.

As with joyful steps they sped,
Saviour, to Thy lowly bed,
There to bend the knee before
Him whom heaven and earth adore,
So may we with willing feet
Ever seek Thy mercy-seat.

As they offered gifts most rare
At Thy cradle rude and bare,
So may we with holy joy,
Pure, and free from sin's alloy,
All our costliest treasures bring,
Christ, to Thee, our Heavenly King.

Holy Jesus, every day
Keep us in the narrow way;
And, when earthly things are past,
Bring our ransomed souls at last
Where they need no star to guide,
Where no clouds Thy glory hide.

In the heavenly country bright
Need they no created light;
Thou its Light, its Joy, its Crown,
Thou its Sun, which goes not down.
There for ever may we sing
Hallelujahs to our King.

As with gladness men of old – Lyrics written by William Chatterton Dix on 6 January (Epiphany) 1859.

Reflect:

The opening lines of *As with gladness...* transport us straight into a key Christmas scene – to the 'men of old' who followed the star from the East in order to meet a special king. But this carol doesn't just narrate the story beautifully for us; it asks for more...

The words invite us to join in with living the story ourselves; into reprising it in our own context. They hold up the 'men of old' as an example for our own lives and involve us in voicing a prayer which asks to repeat their choices. As we sing this carol, we find we are expressing a desire to follow, kneel and give with the same extravagance as those who went before us.

Look through the words of the carol again and see how many elements of this familiar part of the story are changed from narrative or theology into participating, personal action...

We are praying to be led by Jesus into single-hearted focus and pursuit; into submission to Him; and into generous devotion. If we mean this prayer, and seek to live it out, we will find we are led into action.

Following Jesus has never just been about believing stories or creeds. It has always been about love-led action.

Looking back through all the men and women in the Bible and Christian history who have gone before us, there are many outstanding examples who inspire us to get involved; to be active in our devotion and service in ways that can make an extraordinary difference to the world.

The same is true for Embrace the Middle East! It is a microcosm of the whole kingdom. Today's work benefits from the devotion and hard-work of volunteers, supporters and devoted partners in the Middle East and the UK. But it is also made possible – and inspired by the joyful legacy – of 160 years' worth of lives who faithfully loved and served, long before all of us got involved.

Today is International Volunteer Day. What better day to give thanks for all those who have given their time to God and others before us; all those doing so today – here and in the Middle East; and to prayerfully hold our own involvement in His-story before God?

Embrace partner Caritas Jerusalem and volunteers distribute emergency goods.

Photo credit: Virginie Nguyen Hoang

Pray:

Lord Jesus, lead me; be my wholehearted focus. Bring me to my knees and cause me to be generous to you and others, here and across the Middle East. Inspire me by your Word, your Spirit, and the example of many men and women of old in history – and throughout the world today – who have followed, knelt and given so faithfully and extravagantly before me.

Ideas for: inspiring and blessing those who take practical action

• Embrace the Middle East was founded by men and women 'of old'. More than 160 years ago, compassionate people came together to raise funds for the destitute in Turkey – and the rest is history! Spend some time today learning about Embrace's story, from its roots as the Turkish Missions Aid Society to its modern focus on development and advocacy. Visit **www.embraceme.org/our-history** to find out more.

• Pray for all Embrace's volunteers, staff and supporters – and ask God, in His grace, to extend this vital support base for His work in the Middle East today.

O holy night!

Pause and count: how many times you have
seen a depiction of Father Christmas already this year.

Enjoy today's carol:

O holy night! The stars are brightly shining,
It is the night of our dear Saviour's birth.
Long lay the world in sin and error pining,
Till He appeared and the soul felt its worth.
A thrill of hope, the weary world rejoices,
For yonder breaks a new and glorious morn.
Fall on your knees! O hear the angel voices!
O night divine, O night when Christ was born;
O night divine, O night, O night divine.

Led by the light of faith serenely beaming,
With glowing hearts by His cradle we stand.
So led by light of a star sweetly gleaming,
Here come the wise men from the Orient land.
The King of Kings lay thus in lowly manger;
In all our trials born to be our friend.
He knows our need, to our weaknesses no stranger,
Behold your King! Before Him lowly bend!
Behold your King, Before Him lowly bend!

Truly He taught us to love one another;
His law is love and His gospel is peace.
Chains shall He break for the slave is our brother;
And in His name all oppression shall cease.
Sweet hymns of joy in grateful chorus raise we,
Let all within us praise His holy name.
Christ is the Lord! O praise His Name forever,
His power and glory evermore proclaim!
His power and glory evermore proclaim!

O holy night – English lyrics translated and adapted by John Sullivan Dwight from the original French carol, which set the poem "Minuit, chrétiens" (Midnight, Christians) by Placide Cappeau (1808–1877) to music.

A refugee mother and her child at an Embrace-funded health centre in Egypt.

Reflect:

O holy night! again focuses us in on the atmosphere and beauty of that first Christmas night; 'the stars are brightly shining' and we know, straight away, that the stage is being set for something uplifting.

This carol still gets plenty of radio play and is often included on secular Christmas compilation albums. But the third verse – which actually contains a bold, political message – is usually edited out for these contexts. Read it again now...

Among the Christmas card images of dark blue skies, bright stars and simple, white dwellings, a new picture emerges. The holiness of Jesus' coming kingdom is no longer about idyllic beauty; it is about ending oppression and injustice.

It is *our* desire to sentimentalise – not Jesus' message – that is tempted to think that talking about slavery, trafficking, refugees or war is not suitable subject matter for Christmas carols.

This would have been understood well by the original St Nicholas, who is celebrated in Lebanon and Palestine on 6 December with special liturgy and parades. The town of Beit Jala, two kilometres west of Bethlehem, even has St Nicholas as its patron saint.

The man behind the myth was the Bishop of Myra (now in modern-day Turkey). One legend says that he rescued the daughters of a poor man from being sold into slavery as prostitutes by throwing gold balls to their father out of his carriage window.

Just like the frequent editing of *O holy night*, our embellishment of Father Christmas – and even of gift giving at Christmas – has created a lot of glitter around the original kingdom grit of Christ's message. There's nothing wrong with glitter; it's an appropriate accompaniment to joy! Just as long as we don't start telling the grit it's getting in the way...

Pray:

Lord Jesus, teach me to prize others as you do, and to live out your gospel of peace. This Christmas, help me strip back anything that stops me seeing your kingdom's holy priority of chain-breaking, oppression-ending love, and use me to challenge injustice with, and for, you.

Ideas for: beginning a Christmas revolution

- Explore writing (or asking a friend to write) a new third verse for *O holy night!* to include in your church's carol service. It could challenge people to see the relevance of the Christmas message to our responsibility towards refugees from Syria.

- Think about other ways of refocusing your celebrations so that they challenge injustice – for example, read out a story from Embrace magazine in church or at a Christmas gathering, to help those present connect with the experiences of their fellow human beings in the Middle East.

In the bleak mid-winter

Pause and consider:
where you've got to with your Christmas shopping...

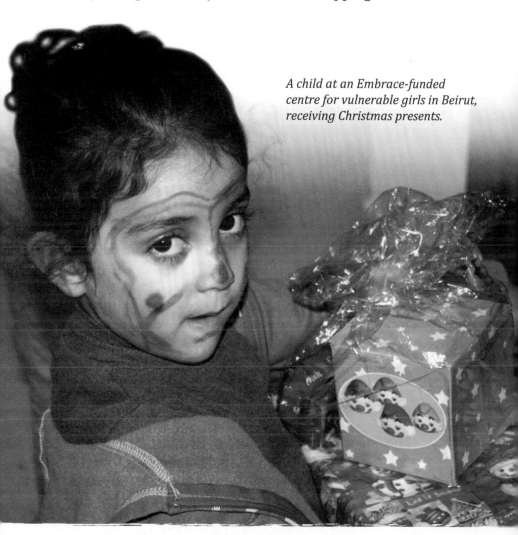

A child at an Embrace-funded centre for vulnerable girls in Beirut, receiving Christmas presents.

31

Enjoy today's carol:

In the bleak mid-winter
Frosty wind made moan,
Earth stood hard as iron,
Water like a stone;
Snow had fallen, snow on snow,
Snow on snow,
In the bleak mid-winter,
Long ago.

Our God, heaven cannot hold Him,
Nor earth sustain;
Heaven and earth shall flee away
When He comes to reign:
In the bleak mid-winter
A stable-place sufficed
The Lord God Almighty,
Jesus Christ.

Angels and archangels
May have gathered there,
Cherubim and seraphim
Thronged the air;
But His mother only,
In her maiden bliss,
Worshipped the Belovèd
With a kiss.

What can I give Him,
Poor as I am?
If I were a shepherd,
I would bring a lamb.
If I were a wise man,
I would do my part,
Yet what I can I give Him –
Give my heart.

In the bleak mid-winter – Lyrics taken from the poem by English poet Christina Rossetti (1830-1894).

Reflect:

In the bleak mid-winter **draws us in by describing a westernised winter scene where the 'earth stood hard as iron'.**

But Christina Rossetti, who wrote the original poem, seems intent on drawing our focus away from the setting for Christ's physical coming towards the hardness, or softness, of our own hearts' response to Him.

Reread the final verse... The words paint the familiar nativity characters again, reminding us of what they brought in worship, but we are in the picture too. What will we give Him?

The poet resolves to give Christ her heart, and so do we, every time we sing it. But what does this mean? And how might we be able to tell if we are actually doing so?

Jesus said: *'where your treasure is, there is your heart...'* (Matthew 6:21). In other words – what outward treasure you have, or how much you bring is not what's important. But *where* you choose to place what you do have is everything.

The shepherds' treasure was a lamb – and it's likely it was proportionately more valuable to them than the gold, frankincense and myrrh were to Jesus' other visitors. But they gave it gladly and joyfully; they placed their treasure with Jesus.

The wise men also chose to locate their treasured riches with Christ; it is clear where their hearts were invested.

How about us? Where will our gifts be placed this Christmas?

It was the Victorians who really created our modern emphasis on sending cards and gifts to each other. It is a beautiful way to celebrate together – and most of us in our culture are rich enough to do it. It is a good thing! But we can easily end up spending more time thinking about giving to each other than we do about giving to God.

Additionally, there are many people, who Jesus counted precious enough to come to earth for, who are in need – around us and in the Middle East. Investing more of our treasure in 'the least' (Matthew 25:40) is one of God's kingdom priorities.

So this Advent, if we truly want to give Jesus more of our hearts, it's worth prayerfully re-examining where our treasure will be placed this Christmas.

Pray:

Lord Jesus, you and your priorities are what I want to spend Advent preparing for. So what can I give you, just as I am? What would it mean to truly give you my heart? Show me who you want me to share with and how to keep you central to my gift giving.

Ideas for: placing your gifts where your heart is

- As you wrap each gift with love and care this Christmas, think about how it reflects Jesus and the things that matter to Him the most. Then pray for the recipient and his or her own Christian journey.

- One practical way you could do this is to choose faith-inspired items, or gifts whose sale benefits people in need. Embrace could help with this – visit **shop.embraceme.org** or browse our print catalogue for a range of beautiful gifts designed to encourage faith in your recipients and to change lives in the Middle East.

Silent night, holy night

Pause and remember again:

just how extraordinary Mary's story really is.

Enjoy today's carol:

Silent night, holy night.
All is calm, all is bright
Round yon Virgin mother and Child;
Holy Infant, so tender and mild,
Sleep in heavenly peace,
Sleep in heavenly peace.

Silent night, holy night.
Shepherds quake at the sight,
Glories stream from heaven afar,
Heavenly hosts sing Alleluia:
Christ, the Saviour is born,
Christ, the Saviour is born.

Silent night, holy night.
Son of God, Love's pure Light
Radiant beams from Thy holy face,
With the dawn of redeeming grace:
Jesus, Lord, at Thy birth,
Jesus, Lord, at Thy birth.

Silent night, holy night – Lyrics translated into English by John Freeman Young in 1859 from the original German words to Stille Nacht, heilige Nacht by Joseph Mohr (1792-1848).

Reflect:

The soaring melody of *Silent night* circles round us and helps weave together the picture the words also evoke; we, like the night, are shushed as we contemplate this most sacred of all first moments between a mother and her child.

Today, Christians within Roman Catholic traditions will be celebrating the Feast of the Immaculate Conception. Differences in belief over some of the specifics of Mary's role mean that there is a vast difference between the amount of focus she receives in various parts of the church. But whatever you believe, revisiting the astonishing events of her story, and looking to her as a model for what it means to live in radical obedience and surrender to God, is always a powerful and inspiring lesson.

When the angel visited her, Mary said a joyful yes to God. As a result of her humble heart, and God's call and favour on her life, she was chosen to nurture God's own son. Even after the trials of Joseph's initial reaction, and in the midst of an illegitimate pregnancy, we find her with her cousin Elizabeth, singing of the great goodness of God and her delight in the way He works. Her concern is for the justice of her people – and all people – over her own life's fulfilment.

God is always preparing the hearts of His followers so they can house His precious work. What might He be asking you to protect and grow next? And are you ready to say a joyful yes to Him?

Embrace's partners across the Middle East provide many examples of individuals who exhibit Mary-like humility; people who have said a joyful yes to housing astonishing works of God-inspired grace in and through their lives.

One example of this is also a namesake for Mary. Sister Maria is a Coptic Christian nun who runs the Salaam Centre, which reaches out to the ostracised 'garbage people' on the outskirts of Cairo, Egypt. In the midst of incredibly difficult circumstances, and others' chaotic lives, Sister Maria helps create a haven that nurtures peace, and transforms many lives.

Pray:

Lord Jesus, teach me as I look back at Mary's story, and look east to Sister Maria's example. Help me to see differently what is possible. Humble my heart so I am ready to say my own joyful yes to every work of your kingdom you long to house in my life for protection and growth.

A full waiting room at the Salaam Centre, Cairo.

Ideas for: considering Mary and Sister Maria throughout today

- Spend some time rereading The Magnificat (Luke 1:46-55) and be freshly inspired by Mary's heart of worship, and her passion for justice.

- Write out Sister Maria's name and place it somewhere you will see it throughout the day. Every time you look at it, offer a short prayer of thanks and blessing over her and all who serve so selflessly through Embrace.

So tender and mild

The Salaam Centre cares for the whole community, but some of the most vulnerable are new mothers and their babies. As well as providing antenatal and postnatal care in its spotless clinic, the centre holds health seminars so women can learn more about nutrition, hygiene, and how to recognise childhood diseases. Importantly, the centre is also a place where those suffering violence at home can find help and support.

While shepherds watched

Pause and reflect: have you ever found it hard
to make peace with someone? What made it so hard?

Enjoy today's carol:

**While shepherds watched
their flocks by night,**
All seated on the ground,
The Angel of the Lord came down,
And glory shone around.

'Fear not,' said he (for mighty dread
Had seized their troubled mind),
'Glad tidings of great joy I bring
To you and all mankind.

*Sheep grazing
in Wadi Qelt,
West Bank.*

'To you in David's
    town this day
Is born of David's line
A Saviour, who is Christ the Lord –
And this shall be the sign:

'The heavenly Babe
    you there shall find
To human view displayed,
All meanly wrapped
    in swaddling bands,
And in a manger laid.'

Thus spake the Seraph,
    and forthwith
Appeared a shining throng
Of angels praising God, who thus
Addressed their joyful song:

'All glory be to God on high,
And to the earth be peace;
Goodwill henceforth
    from heaven to men
Begin and never cease.'

While shepherds watched – Lyrics written by Nahum Tate in 1703.

Reflect:

The shepherds were just there on the hillside doing what they always did – watching their sheep. When suddenly... blazing light. And then – angels!

It must have been a total shock. No wonder what they most needed to hear was 'Fear not'.

The Bible contains hundreds of verses repeating this command. It is something God knows He needs to tell us repeatedly. For The Bible teaches that fear – not hate – is the opposite of love.

The shepherds truly had nothing to be frightened of, because Jesus' birth marked the coming of perfect love. It began a reconciliation process between God and humankind and set off a kingdom chain reaction of new possibilities for goodwill between people.

But how can the earth experience peace when we are still fearful of God and each other?

Fear is not just the opposite of love; it is also the enemy of peace.

Rebuilding communities after decades of conflict and distrust is challenging. It requires individuals paying the great personal price of forgiving and letting go. But it is possible. This is the hard work of peacebuilding.

It's a work that Embrace's partner Musalaha (which means reconciliation) knows well. Their mission is to bring individual Palestinian women together with individual Israeli women – face-to-face.

Friendships are formed and mutual comfort is offered. Before long, common ground becomes clear, and the revelations of new relationships and deeper perceptions begin to lead to new commitments to reconcile.

In time, whole communities will move towards each other. All because a few precious hearts began to hear 'fear not' loud enough to take those first, tentative steps forward. And then joined their voices in chorus, calling for peace and goodwill to both Palestinians and Israelis.

To the earth be peace

Musalaha also runs activities for young people from Israeli and Palestinian backgrounds to get to know each other. One participant, a teenage girl from Bethlehem, told us: 'I knew that Musalaha gathers Jews and Palestinians so I wanted to go to learn how to come closer to each other and to learn reconciliation rather than hate. Musalaha also gathers us to have fun, to help us make new friends and to learn from God's word.'

Pray:

Lord Jesus, the angels said 'fear not!' as they announced your Christmas gift of reconciliation, all wrapped up in light. Help me lay down any fear that gets in the way of my relationships and do the same – individual by individual, community by community – in Israel, Palestine and everywhere in the Middle East that so desperately needs peace and goodwill to come.

Ideas for: ending fear together

- Pray for the work of Musalaha – for an end to fear in each and every woman involved, and for their new friendships to pave the way for transformed relationships between Israeli and Palestinian communities.

- There are many friendships of peace being established between Israelis and Palestinians all over the world – connected through prayer, generosity, awareness raising or campaigning. But fear creeps in internationally too and prevents others from getting involved. Telling good news stories of peace helps to change this. Tell your friends, or people at church this Sunday, about Musalaha's ministry. Explain that when we confront fear with love, peace and goodwill are born again for everyone.

We three kings of Orient are

Pause and ask yourself:

how and where do I have influence over others?

Enjoy today's carol:

We three kings of Orient are,
Bearing gifts we travel afar,
Field and fountain, moor and mountain,
Following yonder star:
O star of wonder, star of night,
Star with royal beauty bright,
Westward leading, still proceeding,
Guide us to thy perfect light.

Born a King on Bethlehem's plain,
Gold I bring to crown Him again:
King for ever, ceasing never,
Over us all to reign.
O star of wonder...

Frankincense to offer have I;
Incense owns a Deity nigh:
Prayer and praising, all are raising,
Worship Him, God most high.
O star of wonder...

Myrrh is mine: its bitter perfume
Breathes a life of gathering gloom;
Sorrowing, sighing, bleeding, dying,
Sealed in the stone-cold tomb.
O star of wonder...

Glorious now, behold Him arise,
King and God and sacrifice.
Heaven sings, 'Alleluia!'
'Alleluia!' the earth replies.
O star of wonder...

We three kings of Orient are – Lyrics written by Rev. John Henry Hopkins in 1857.

Palestinian youth stand on a rooftop in Aida Refugee Camp overlooking the separation wall and snow-covered olive groves on the other side. Bethlehem, West Bank

Photo credit: Ryan Rodrick Beiler

Reflect:

Kings, wise men, Magi – many names and theories surround the visitors described in Matthew 2:1-12. But there are three things made very clear in this account.

The first is we actually don't know how many of them there were. The second is we know they were from the East. And the third is they were certainly influential.

They had the wealth to give costly gold, frankincense and myrrh; the freedom and finances to be able to lay down their responsibilities and travel a significant distance. And they had the gifting or education to interpret a new star in the night sky, murky motives in powerful rulers and the confusing reality of discovering a king in a manger. They also had a commanding enough presence to achieve an audience with Herod.

How they chose to use this influence in the Christmas story is striking. Everything – wealth, time, gifting, education, presence – was spent on worshipfully pursuing the true king of all and to protecting Him from the jealous anger of Israel's compromised ruler.

Most of us underestimate, rather than overestimate, our potential influence to bring comfort, joy or transformation.

Nader Abu Amsha is the Director of the YMCA in Beit Sahour, Bethlehem. This is a responsible position but he could have had so much more. As a young man, Nader gave up the opportunity to study physics at a university in the USA. Instead he stayed in Palestine to train in counselling so that he could use his intellect to challenge Israel's occupation through peaceful means – and so he could help other young Palestinian men.

One of these young men was Khalid. Like Nader, he was detained by the Israeli army as a teenager. In Khalid's case, his detention lasted nine months, which led to him losing his place at school. The future looked hopeless. But thanks to Nader and the YMCA's influence, Khalid was trained to fix mobile phones through one of the centre's vocational courses and is now running a successful hardware business of his own in Hebron.

Pray:

Lord Jesus, give me the wisdom of your first Eastern visitors so that I too may use my influence to worship you and protect the vulnerable around me and across the Middle East. Shine a light on all you have given me – wealth, time, gifting, education, insight – and lead me to the way you would have me use each of these things this Christmas and beyond.

Ideas for: celebrating transformational influence

- Pray for Nader, Khalid and everyone at the YMCA. Pray also for all the politicians and policymakers who have power to effect change, so that no more young men go through the same experiences.

- Today is the UN Day for Human Rights – a day designed to encourage the international community to speak up for those whose rights are being abused. How could you use your influence, talents and connections to raise awareness of the difficulties detainees are facing? Could you write to your MP, speak up about it on social media, or tell friends about Khalid's story?

The holly and the ivy

Pause and imagine:
a holly tree, or some holly themed decorations...

Enjoy today's carol:

The holly and the ivy,
When they are both full grown,
Of all the trees that are in the wood,
The holly bears the crown:
Oh, the rising of the sun
And the running of the deer,
The playing of the merry organ,
Sweet singing in the choir.

The holly bears a blossom,
As white as lily flower,
And Mary bore sweet Jesus Christ,
To be our sweet Saviour:
Oh, the rising of the sun...

The holly bears a berry,
As red as any blood,
And Mary bore sweet Jesus Christ
To do poor sinners good:
Oh, the rising of the sun...

The holly bears a prickle,
As sharp as any thorn,
And Mary bore sweet Jesus Christ
On Christmas day in the morn:
Oh, the rising of the sun...

The holly bears a bark,
As bitter as any gall,
And Mary bore sweet Jesus Christ
For to redeem us all:
Oh, the rising of the sun...

The holly and the ivy,
When they are both full grown,
Of all the trees that are in the wood,
The holly bears the crown:
Oh, the rising of the sun...

The holly and the ivy – Lyrics taken from the traditional British folk carol.

Reflect:

On 2 December, *O Christmas tree! O Christmas tree!* led us to reflect on the symbol of faithfulness that the fir tree provides. Today's carol draws our attention to two more evergreens, although it is really just focused on the holly.

Again appropriated for Christmas celebrations from pagan traditions, holly is given a religious makeover, creating a meditation inspired by different aspects of its growth.

The holly's white blossom can remind us of the purity of God's Son; the red berry evokes the blood He spilled to redeem us; the prickles lead the writer to reference the crown of thorns; and the bark is compared to bitter gall – which was offered to Jesus to drink on the cross.

The melody trips along with the dancing lilt a true carol always establishes. But the lyrics lead us to look beyond celebrating the birth of a baby, to the death of a man on another tree that brought us life. A death that set in motion a new kingdom of justice and peace.

Pause for a moment and let the holly lead you to worship and thank Christ again...

The olive is a much more familiar tree in the landscape Jesus walked in. And this tree is rich in meaning too. It symbolises peace everywhere. But in Palestine, it also represents rootedness in the land.

Olive trees have been a major source of income for Palestinians for hundreds of years – covering half of all agricultural land, and helping to support 100,000 families. But since the 1967 occupation of the West Bank, hundreds of thousands of olive trees – farmed by the same families for generations – have been uprooted to make way for Israeli settlements.

Embrace and its partners are bringing comfort and keeping hope alive by planting and replanting olive trees in Palestinian areas at risk of confiscation. Since 2014, Embrace supporters have sponsored over 6,000 trees, ensuring the olive can continue to bring life to those who desperately need it.

This Christmas – when you see the evergreens that bring life and colour into your home – could you make space to remember the olive tree too, and to pray for those who cultivate it in Palestine today?

A grove of olive trees at Sepphoris near Nazareth.

Pray:

Lord Jesus, thank you that the holly tree can remind me of your cross. Lead me to remember this Christmas that you came for Easter; to give your life so we could have peace with God. Keep reminding me of the olive tree too, and bless Embrace's work through the Olive Tree Project, so that together we can all be part of growing peace and justice in the Middle East.

Ideas for: extending the olive's branches

- Place an olive tree, or an item made from olive wood, among your Christmas decorations and use it as a prompt to pray for the Palestinian olive farmers.

- If you are ordering gifts from Embrace and want to make sure they arrive before Christmas, don't leave it too late! You could consider buying some olive products that will support Palestinian farmers, or purchasing our very special 'Sponsor an olive tree' gift for someone you love. Visit **shop.embraceme.org** or call **01227 811646** to order.

It came upon the midnight clear

Pause and remember:

the loudest music you have ever heard... where were you?

Enjoy today's carol:

It came upon the midnight clear
That glorious song of old,
From angels bending near the earth,
To touch their harps of gold;
'Peace on the earth, goodwill to men,
From heaven's all-gracious King!'
The world in solemn stillness lay
To hear the angels sing.

Still through the cloven skies they come,
With peaceful wings unfurled,
And still their heavenly music floats
O'er all the weary world;
Above its sad and lonely plains
They bend on heavenly wing,
And ever o'er its Babel sounds
The blessèd angels sing.

Yet, with the woes of sin and strife,
The world has suffered long;
Beneath the angels' strain have rolled
Two thousand years of wrong;
And man, at war with man, hears not
The love-song which they bring:
Oh, hush the noise, ye men of strife,
And hear the angels sing.

For lo! the days are hastening on,
By prophet bards foretold,
When, with the ever circling years,
Comes round the age of gold;
When peace shall over all the earth
Its ancient splendours fling,
And the whole world send back the song
Which now the angels sing!

It came upon the midnight clear – Lyrics written by Edmund Sears in (1810-1876).

Reflect:

It came upon the midnight clear **was written in December 1845 by a vicar in Massachusetts who was well aware of the tensions already building towards the American Civil War in his country.**

Now, as then, it takes little artistic license to imagine 'man at war with man' or to envisage the noise of 'strife' being so loud that it makes it hard to tune into the strain of peace that is still echoing the news that Christ has been born.

Conflict is one of the most familiar refrains of modern and ancient history. Our ability to compete, attack and fight transcends all cultures, climates and ages.

We do not need to realise again how relevant the problem voiced by this carol is today – across the world and within the Middle East particularly.

But we desperately need the comfort of the conclusion it leads us towards, which encourages us to take heart. One day, peace will be complete – and it shall 'fling' its 'ancient splendours' over the earth and meet a song there that picks up its own refrain.

We also need to remember that there is really an extra verse needed in this carol too. For – thank God – there are those who already try to 'send back the song which now the angels sing'. There are people now who strive to build peace in difficult places; people who want to harmonise with kingdom come today.

Some of these people strive to change the big picture, such as those campaigning for an end to the Gaza blockade, which has led to Gaza having one of the highest employment rates in the world, creating tension and despair among its youthful population.

Some champion peacebuilding activities that help individuals affected by conflict now, such as the YMCA in Gaza. Here, around 150 young people play sport which helps them exercise, socialise and inspire each other to change their communities.

No, we will never be completely free from war until Christ returns. But yes, we can build peace now – lending our voices and lives to join the angels and people already singing this new, extra verse of the angels' song.

Boys pose for a picture in Shuja'lyya, a Gaza neighbourhood which bore the brunt of some of the most intense air attacks during the 2014 war.

Pray:

Lord Jesus, make me one of those who strain to hear the song of peace, whether it is sung by angels above or men and women below. And show me how my life can echo this song by building your kingdom of peace now.

Ideas for: swelling the harmonic chorus

- The world needs more reminders of peace than of war. When you are next talking with friends, family, colleagues or other church members about conflict, take some time to tell a story of someone who is already joining the angels' song of peace.

- As well as sharing stories of peace, we need to help write them. Pray for the YMCA and everyone involved in peacebuilding work – you can learn more about Gaza by visiting **www.embraceme.org** and typing Gaza into the search box to look for recent updates.

A land that has suffered long

The Gaza Strip is a Palestinian territory of just 141 square miles – smaller than the Isle of Wight. Yet it is home to some 1.85 million people, who cannot freely travel across the Israeli and Egyptian borders. Conflict, fuel shortages, power cuts, lack of imported goods and medicines, overcrowding and high unemployment have left many destitute. Embrace's partners are some of the few remaining Christians in Gaza, but their provision of healthcare, education and training has a huge positive impact.

Good King Wenceslas

Pause and think: of your favourite Christmas foods and who you are planning to eat dinner with on 25 December this year.

Enjoy today's carol:

Good King Wenceslas look'd out
On the Feast of Stephen,
When the snow lay round about,
Deep, and crisp and even;
Brightly shone the moon that night,
Though the frost was cruel,
When a poor man came in sight,
Gathering winter fuel.

'Hither page, and stand by me,
If thou know'st it telling,
Yonder peasant, who is he?
Where and what his dwelling?'
'Sire, he lives a good league hence,
Underneath the mountain,
Right against the forest fence,
By Saint Agnes' fountain.'

'Bring me flesh and bring me wine,
Bring me pine logs hither;
Thou and I will see him dine,
When we bear them thither.'
Page and monarch, forth they went,
Forth they went together,
Through the rude wind's wild lament
And the bitter weather.

'Sire, the night is darker now,
And the wind blows stronger;
Fails my heart, I know not how;
I can go no longer.'
'Mark my footsteps, good my page,
Tread thou in them boldly;
Thou shalt find the winter's rage
Freeze thy blood less coldly.'

In his master's steps he trod,
Where the snow lay dinted;
Heat was in the very sod
Which the saint had printed.
Therefore, Christians all, be sure,
Wealth or rank possessing,
Ye who now will bless the poor
Shall yourselves find blessing.

Good King Wenceslas – Lyrics written by John Mason Neale in 1853.

Reflect:

Today's carol tells a story, or perhaps more accurately, a parable.

St Stephen's Day is the day after Christmas, so it's effectively the equivalent of the modern Boxing Day. Good King Wenceslas (a fictional character inspired by the true story of tenth century Bohemian duke, Vaclav) is looking out at the bitterly cold weather.

We're not told what he would see if he stayed looking at what was around him inside, but we can presume given it is a 'feast' and he is a man of position, that he is surrounded by warmth and comfort. It doesn't seem much of a stretch to visualise tables groaning with delicious food and drink.

By contrast, outside, a poor man is walking through the snow, looking for scraps of wood to burn.

King Wenceslas is clearly struck by the desperate situation of the man and asks his page who the 'peasant' is. Reflection leads to action and the king and the page go out together, laden down with gifts from their feast (meat, wine and pine logs) and determined to extend their comfort to him despite the long distance and bad weather ahead. When the page struggles to keep going and begins to falter, his master helps him.

Then, the parable underlines its moral, and we are invited to play out the next chapter of the story ourselves through the closing four lines of the carol.

This last verse underlines the unifying effect of Jesus. He came for every section of society and His love is best exemplified, and His person best worshipped, when those who have plenty and those who don't are brought together in a new, kingdom-based equality.

Of course it is food for thought what happens next in the story... do the king and his page return to their comfort and leave the poor man in his dwelling?

Pray:

Lord Jesus, help me to look out beyond my walls and to share my feasting generously on Christmas Day and every day. Thank you for all who seek to 'bless the poor'. Grow your church's understanding of what it means to love like you, and to worship in a way that builds your kingdom's equality; until no one is ever left out in the cold.

Ideas for: breaking down barriers

- Life-changing generosity is experienced every day through Embrace's bursary scheme, which provides disadvantaged children with an education in Christian schools across the West Bank and Gaza. Pray for every child who receives this gift.

Treading boldly

Embrace provides bursaries for children at 17 Christian schools in East Jerusalem, the West Bank and Gaza – children like Karim, whose father died suddenly of a heart attack, leaving the family without a breadwinner. Karim lives with his disabled mother and two sisters in one small room. But he dreams of being an aerospace engineer; he loves science and maths. His bursary from Embrace enables him to go to a school that supports his dream, so that even when things are difficult, Karim can keep looking at the stars.

Go tell it on the mountain

Pause to remember: when you first began to be concerned for people living in the Middle East, or how you originally came across Embrace's work.

Enjoy today's carol:

Go tell it on the mountain,
Over the hills and everywhere,
Go tell it on the mountain,
Our Jesus Christ is born.

When I was a seeker
I sought both night and day,
I asked the Lord to help me,
And he showed me the way.

Go tell it on the mountain...

He made me a watchman
Upon a city wall,
And if I am a Christian,
I am the least of all.

Go tell it on the mountain...

Go tell it on the mountain – Lyrics taken from the traditional African American spiritual song, compiled by John Wesley Work, Jr., at least as early as 1865.

Reflect:

There is a lot of movement involved in the Christmas story. Multiple locations provide backdrops for each of the key characters, and everyone makes significant journeys beyond their comfort zones.

The Son of God comes from heaven to be born on earth. Gabriel and whole hosts of angels also descend to another realm. Mary and Joseph travel from Nazareth to Bethlehem, and then from Bethlehem to Egypt with Jesus. The shepherds leave their flocks and hills; the wise men come from the East...

... all so Christ can bring His message of good news to the poor.

The words of today's carol – as well as its joyful rhythm – pick up on this movement. But they argue it is not just the characters of the Nativity who are called to move; we must 'go' too. The story we are singing is not one to just hear and receive for ourselves. It's one to join in with and spread the word about to others. Jesus being born means there is good news for everyone; everywhere!

Go tell it on the mountain started life during the mid-19th century as an African American spiritual song, designed to keep collective hope alive in the hearts and communities of those still waiting for their freedom.

Limestone cliffs in the Judean Mountains.

In the 21st century we still need its reminders. There are people beyond our churches who have forgotten the true Christmas story. There are people in our congregations, including ourselves sometimes, who have forgotten that Jesus came to move us all beyond our comfort zones. There are people across the Middle East longing to hear a song of freedom rise that challenges and changes injustice again. And there are people you know who don't yet realise how they could be part of bringing good news to the Middle East today.

It's time to move; we have a lot of 'telling' still to do...

Pray:

Lord Jesus, fill my heart with courage, move my feet beyond what is familiar and open my mouth to tell your joyful story. Not just the Nativity tableau the carols paint but the loving 'why?' and 'what for?' which led you – the Son of God – to move heaven and earth to be and bring good news to the poor. And to tell me – just one in the billions you came for – to live and go and tell like you.

Ideas for: telling it everywhere

- Ask friends, family, colleagues or church members what their favourite Christmas carol is and then share about these reflections. You could even show them your favourite tiding so far...

- If you're writing a round robin letter for your cards or posting a Christmas message on social media, you could include something about your concern for the Middle East and how getting involved with Embrace has helped you do something positive to bring comfort and joy to the people living there.

Angels, from the realms of glory

Pause and consider: the types of emotions that come to mind for most people in the UK when they hear the phrase 'the Middle East'.

Enjoy today's carol:

Angels, from the realms of glory,
Wing your flight o'er all the earth;
Ye who sang creation's story
Now proclaim Messiah's birth:
Come and worship
Christ, the new-born King.
Come and worship,
Worship Christ, the new-born King.

Shepherds in the fields abiding,
Watching o'er your flocks by night,
God with us is now residing;
Yonder shines the Infant Light:
Come and worship...

Sages, leave your contemplations;
Brighter visions beam afar;
Seek the great Desire of Nations;
Ye have seen His natal star;
Come and worship...

Saints before the altar bending,
Watching long in hope and fear,
Suddenly the Lord, descending,
In His temple shall appear:
Come and worship...

Angels, from the realms of glory – Lyrics written by James Montgomery in 1816.

Reflect:

Angels, from the realms of glory is a call to worship, as the refrain that repeats at the end of each verse makes clear.

It addresses a series of characters – moving outwards again from key individuals in the Nativity story to include us too – and calling them all to the same response: devotion to Jesus.

In each case, every person or group addressed is interrupted in the middle of something. They are all summoned to leave their existing, important work to come and do something even better... The angels are urged to upgrade the subject of their song from creation to Christ; the shepherds to leave their fields behind; the 'sages' or wise men to put down their contemplation; and the saints must leave their prayers... for they have been answered!

The saints need to change gear from intercession to joyful adoration – because Christ has come. Can you imagine how strange it would be if they kept soberly praying for the Messiah to come throughout the celebration of all they were asking for having come to pass?

Sometimes we can be so busy 'bending' before the altar 'watching long in hope and fear' that we neglect to notice quite how many of our prayers have been joyfully answered whilst we've been on our knees. We can get so used to carrying a deep concern at the challenges facing the nations of the Middle East that we forget to pause and look back at what communities there have already overcome.

For example, the lives of women, and their families and whole communities, have been radically changed forever by Embrace's partner, Think and Do, who run 'Life Schools' for women who missed out on education as children.

One in three women in Egypt are illiterate and this impacts everything in their daily life – from reading signs and bus numbers to getting a fair price at market. But Fayza and her friends are no longer part of this statistic. Now they can sign their names when they vote, avoid being cheated, and find their way around with independence and confidence.

Women learning to read at 'Life School'.

Pray:

Lord Jesus, I want to be one who watches and prays for the people who are on your heart. But help me never to be so focused on mourning injustice that I forget to celebrate when it is overcome. Christ, the new-born King has come and His new-born mercies have been answering prayers daily ever since. Today, I am ready to leave even my remaining concerns for the Middle East to express my joy at all you have done there already.

Ideas for: increasing your sense of celebration

- Try to think of – or jot down – as many breakthrough stories from the Middle East as you can. These might be big-picture changes or some of the individual lives and Embrace projects that you have read about in this book over the last couple of weeks. Spend some time rejoicing and thanking God for them.

- Think about any acts of service that you will be doing over the Christmas period – how can you make sure you aren't so busy with these that you miss making time to truly celebrate and praise Jesus for his coming?

Once in royal David's city

Pause and think about:

what you think constitutes a good childhood…
and what makes a good mother.

Enjoy today's carol:

Once in royal David's city
Stood a lowly cattle-shed,
Where a mother laid her baby
In a manger for His bed.
Mary was that mother mild,
Jesus Christ her little child.

He came down to earth from heaven,
Who is God and Lord of all,
And His shelter was a stable,
And His cradle was a stall:
With the poor and mean and lowly
Lived on earth our Saviour holy.

And through all His wondrous
  childhood
He would honour and obey,
Love and watch the lowly maiden,
In whose gentle arms He lay.
Christian children all must be
Mild, obedient, good as He.

For He is our childhood's pattern,
Day by day like us He grew;
He was little, weak and helpless,
Tears and smiles like us He knew;
And He feeleth for our sadness,
And He shareth in our gladness.

And our eyes at last shall see Him,
Through His own redeeming love;
For that Child, so dear and gentle,
Is our Lord in heaven above;
And He leads His children on
To the place where He is gone.

Not in that poor lowly stable,
With the oxen standing by,
We shall see Him, but in heaven,
Set at God's right hand on high;
When like stars His children
  crowned
All in white shall wait around.

Once in royal David's city – Lyrics written by Cecil Frances Alexander (1818-1895).

Reflect:

Every time you read these words, it's hard not to imagine it... It's the opening of nine lessons and carols and a child's pure voice sounds the opening verse's solo. And all in a rushed, hushed stillness, we're transported again – through the gentle pictures of the lyrics and the sweet fragility of that pure sound – to the wonder of Mary stooping down to lay her tiny son in the 'manger for His bed'.

Once in royal David's city charts Jesus' development from helpless baby, through His 'wondrous childhood' not just to adulthood, but to the time when His whole redeeming work is finished, and we are united with Him in eternity.

Mary didn't just have a role in carrying Jesus through pregnancy and nurturing Him in infancy, she was there offering support throughout His childhood. It is what all good mothers hope to do.

The vocational skills workshop at Al-Kafaàt.

Today there are many people across the Middle East whose childhoods did not receive this kind of mothering. But there is always the possibility of comfort and nurture being offered by others.

Jesus said true 'mothers and brothers' can be found throughout the family of God – they are those who hear His word and put it into action (see Luke 8:21).

As a baby, Sabaha contracted meningitis and was left with mild learning disabilities as a result. This led to neglect and abuse in her early years. Some 20 years later, she still remembers vividly the loneliness she felt.

But the Al-Kafaàt Foundation in Beirut, Lebanon, is a place of love that provides a true sense of home and family for people like Sabaha. They took her in aged five and she still has a permanent home there. She even works in their vocational training workshop now.

She says: *'At Al-Kafaàt I found affection.'*

Each of us – Embrace's partners, staff, volunteers, supporters and those who remember the work in prayer – plays a different part in helping children and vulnerable adults like Sabaha find places where they can be joyfully nurtured through childhood. Whatever we contribute, we become part of their family as a result.

Pray:

Lord Jesus, every time I hear a solo voice sound those words, 'Once in royal David's city' help me to remember the priceless worth of each child, wherever they are. Thank you for every family – including yours – that nurtures children well. And thank you for everyone who steps up to comfort and care for those with fractured childhoods across the Middle East. Bless and strengthen them, and help the children in their care to receive an abiding sense of love as a treasured part of your family.

Ideas for: remembering the Middle East's vulnerable children

- Each time you see children locally during the next few days, pray for all the children receiving care, support or counselling from Embrace's partners in the Middle East. Ask God for love, wisdom and resources for these projects so that the orphans and other vulnerable children in their care can flourish.

- Visit Embrace's website at **www.embraceme.org** and search for Al-Kafaàt to find out about the huge variety of work across its seven different sites around Beirut. Then, each day during the current week, choose one of these centres to pray for.

Our childhood's pattern

The Al-Kafaàt Foundation has been an Embrace partner for more than 60 years! Right from the beginning, it has championed the right of disabled people to gain education and training, and to be respected as valued members of society. Children often arrive at Al-Kafaàt from situations where they haven't had a chance to develop to their full potential – Al-Kafaàt changes that pattern of low expectations and helps them thrive.

Joy to the world

Pause and think about:

what joy is and how it feels to experience it.

Enjoy today's carol:

Joy to the world, the Lord has come;
Let earth receive her King.
Let every heart prepare Him room,
And heav'n and nature sing,
And heav'n and nature sing,
And heaven and heaven and nature sing.

Joy to the world! The Saviour reigns;
Let us our songs employ;
While fields and floods, rocks, hills and plains
Repeat the sounding joy,
Repeat the sounding joy,
Repeat, repeat the sounding joy.

He rules the world with truth and grace,
And makes the nations prove
The glories of His righteousness,
And wonders of His Love,
And wonders of His Love,
And wonders, and wonders of His Love.

Joy to the world – Lyrics written by Isaac Watts and first published by him in 1719.

Reflect:

Today's tiding is all about joy! We have reached the third Sunday of Advent and many western Christian denominations celebrate this as 'Gaudete Sunday'.

Traditionally, Advent was much more about fasting than preparing for the coming feast. But on Gaudete Sunday, the focus on repentant preparation for the King – in his past, present and final coming – was paused for a day of celebration.

Gaudete means 'rejoice' in Latin and the focus of readings in churches following the lectionary will have all considered the concept of Christian joy.

In his book *Here and Now*, Henri Nouwen says that while happiness is dependent on external conditions, joy is *'the experience of knowing that you are unconditionally loved and that nothing – sickness, failure, emotional distress, oppression, war, or even death – can take that love away...'*

He continues, *'I remember the most painful times of my life as times in which I became aware of a spiritual reality much larger than myself, a reality that allowed me to live the pain with hope... Joy does not simply happen to us. We have to choose joy and keep choosing it every day.'*

For all we try to look forward to Christmas in Advent, it is also always behind us. He has come! We are always the people who *have seen*. There is still darkness, but we can no longer be in any doubt about the presence of the greater light (see Isaiah 9). Even in the midst of the most desperate circumstances, we see people courageously stand up for hope, justice and freedom. Unshakeable joy can fuel us all to take heart again, and to keep working for change with persistent hope.

Joy to the world! Joy to the Middle East! Joy even to Syria!

A mother and her baby sheltering in a school in Gaza during the conflict, summer 2014.

Photo credit: Virginie Nguyen Hoang

Pray:

Joy to my heart! Our Saviour reigns! Rejoice – and then rejoice again – repeat it, sound it, sing it loud. Joy to the troubled, the distressed, the oppressed, the frightened and the poor; for the Light of the World still shines and His kingdom of hope, justice and freedom is always increasing; in hearts, lives and nations all across the world.

Ideas for: repeating the sounding joy

- Take a paper and pen and spend some time writing down everything you are thankful for – rejoice in who God is, what He has done through Jesus, and the richness of life.

- *'Even in the midst of the most desperate circumstances, we see people courageously stand up for hope, justice and freedom.'* Thank God for Embrace's staff, partners and supporters who are doing just this. And pray especially for all aid workers, war correspondents, residents and refugees in, and from, Syria.

The wonders of His love

Embrace has been working with Syrian refugees since the beginning of the devastating conflict in 2011. Our partners seek out those who are hardest to reach – people living in the most isolated areas, and those who are too frightened to register with large aid agencies. We provide food, blankets, mattresses, fuel, nappies and much more – showing the love of Christ through practical action for those in need.

O come, all ye faithful

Pause and look: at your diary, or think through the week ahead and all you plan to do before Christmas.

Enjoy today's carol:

O come, all ye faithful,
Joyful and triumphant,
Come ye, O come ye to Bethlehem;
Come and behold Him,
Born the King of angels:
O come, let us adore Him,
O come, let us adore Him,
O come, let us adore Him,
Christ the Lord!

God of God,
Light of light,
Lo! He abhors not the Virgin's womb;
Very God,
Begotten, not created:
O come, let us adore Him...

Sing, choirs of angels,
Sing in exultation,
Sing, all ye citizens of heaven above;
Glory to God
In the highest:
O come, let us adore Him...

Yea, Lord, we greet Thee,
Born this happy morning;
Jesus, to Thee be glory given;
Word of the Father,
Now in flesh appearing:
O come, let us adore Him...

O come, all ye faithful – Lyrics translated into English by Frederick Oakeley in 1841 from the original Latin (Adeste Fideles) which has been attributed to various authors, including John Francis Wade (1711–1786).

Reflect:

O, come, all ye faithful opens with, and repeats, a persistent call to worship. You could choose to hear it as an invitation or a command, but either way it leads us to focus on the very centre of Christmas – Christ.

Come to Bethlehem; come and 'behold Him'; come and consider the baby who is also the 'God of God' and 'Light of light'.

In less traditional churches where modern songs and choruses are sung in a freer style, and often used more than hymns, Christmas can present a challenge. Everyone wants to sing carols of course, but this actually means moving substantially away from their less formal songs and usual approach. It is simply accepted that the carol service will have to function differently…

But not when it's time for *O come, all ye faithful*, because so much space is created by this carol's incredibly simple refrain.

A family walk towards their refugee camp in the Bekaa Valley, Lebanon.

In these settings, you may hear this refrain repeated more, or used a number of times with different words that scan to the same tune, such as 'for He alone is worthy' or 'we'll give Him all the glory'. You may have sung these variations yourself. Sometimes, all can fall very quiet at this point, and the pace of the service slows and stills until everyone in the room seems to become focused solely on Jesus… Even the beautiful poetry describing the focus of our adoration is stripped back, so people can just…adore.

All traditions can act as gateways to joyful praise and wonder-filled adoration. But today it's helpful for us to consider the power of simplicity and space – not just in songs, but in our whole lives. We are privileged to have rich traditions and beautiful poetry at Christmas, but sometimes even these can get in the way of accessing those still, spacious moments of wonder. Moments where we can simply adore the one who is Joy.

Pray:

Lord Jesus, help me slow down. Show me where I need less noise, less activity, fewer words or fewer things. Because I want to make space to just come and adore you, Christ my Lord.

Ideas for: making space for wonder

- This is a busy week for most of us – but is there anything you could 'edit out' to create extra space where you can simply come and adore Christ in prayer?

- Noura, a Syrian refugee with a young family, left her home in Raqqa and fled to Lebanon. When she arrived with nothing, Lebanese Christians brought her some basic everyday items to help the family get by. Noura was moved to tears of thanksgiving – the loss of all her possessions made these simple gifts so meaningful. Is there something you could leave out of your celebrations this Christmas? Then, every time you miss it, give thanks for all that you have, inspired by the gratitude and joy expressed by families like Noura's.

All ye citizens

Across the Middle East, people are uprooted from their homes and cast adrift in a dangerous world. Fleeing from war, Syrians cross the borders with nothing but the clothes on their backs. In Gaza, the West Bank and Lebanon, generations of Palestinians survive in permanent refugee camps, separated from their ancestral soil. Refugees from Sudan and Somalia trek hundreds of miles in fear for their lives, towards a safer but difficult existence in Cairo. Our partners reach out the hand of welcome to all, and retain the hope that one day every displaced and despairing person will be a joyful citizen of a peaceful world.

Ding dong! merrily on high

Pause and ask yourself:

what baking smells most make you feel like Christmas is coming?

Enjoy today's carol:

Ding dong! merrily on high
In heaven the bells are ringing;
Ding dong! verily the sky
Is riv'n with angels singing.
Gloria, Hosanna in excelsis!

E'en so here below, below,
Let steeple bells be swungen,
And i-o, i-o, i-o,
By priest and people sungen.
Gloria, Hosanna in excelsis!

Pray you, dutifully prime
Your matin chimes, ye ringers;
May you beautifully rime
Your evetime song, ye singers.
Gloria, Hosanna in excelsis!

Ding dong! merrily on high – Lyrics by George Ratcliffe Woodward (1848–1934), first published in 1924.

Reflect:

We're here! The final week of anticipation has started...

Many schools have broken up and, if there aren't too many preparations left, a sense of celebration is in the air. Today's carol fits the mood... let the bells ring, let everyone sing. *'Let everything that breathes praise the Lord!' (Psalm 150:6). And let them do it merrily! 'Gloria, Hosanna in excelsis!'.*

A woman baking in her home in Egypt.

Yesterday we considered how some of the busyness and traditions of the Christmas period can make it difficult to find – or make – the space to simply adore.

But today we're celebrating the fact that it is also completely fitting that everything good should be harnessed in worship of God, and His coming. Christmas is a feast! And there is something total and multi-sensory about the way we celebrate it that is wonderfully appropriate.

The ancient Jewish prayer, the Shema (Deuteronomy 6:4-5) tells us to love the Lord our God with all our heart, soul and might, and Jesus tells us to do the same (Matthew 22:37-38). He was frequently to be found feasting. Celebration is as much a part of God's ordained order as fasting is – perhaps actually more so.

Our eyes take in the decorations and lights; our ears and voices enjoy the carols; we feel presents to imagine what they are and luxuriate by our firesides; we savour the taste of our Christmas dinner and treats; and we inhale a gorgeous spread of roast dinner, pine forest, cloves, cinnamon, orange and more...

And that is just UK traditions. If we look around the world, we can see expressions of Christmas joy translated into a huge variety of sights, songs and smells.

In Egypt, for example, Christmas smells of 'kahk'. This is a rich, buttery treat – its name simply means 'biscuit' in Arabic – which can be served plain or filled with delicious mixes of dates, walnuts or pistachios.

It is right that the best foods, music and decorations come out. It is fitting – our duty and our joy – to praise Him with everything at our disposal, wherever we are!

Pray:

Lord Jesus, let me merrily join in with people all over the world in the myriad ways we have found to say Christ is with us! In worship; in baking, eating, decorating, wrapping and giving; help me use every sense to celebrate the wonder of who you are, what you have done and how much you love your world.

Ideas for: involving every sense in your celebrations

- Saying goodbye to an old tradition can create space for getting back to the real meaning of Christmas. But so can adding something fresh that brings the message of joy alive in a new way. Why not try your hand at baking kahk and bring the aroma of Egyptian celebrations into your home? You can find recipes online.

- The smooth surface of a carefully crafted olive wooden holding cross can help you focus on prayer and spending some time in the moment with God. Embrace offers holding crosses made in Bethlehem – find out more at **shop.embraceme.org**

May you beautifully rime

Creativity is at the heart of so much of our partners' work. Through art, music, dance and cookery, people find meaning and hope. At the Shams el Birr Centre in Egypt, young people with disabilities can learn to play musical instruments, and the centre is often filled with song. At Al-Kafaàt in Lebanon, vibrant paintings decorate the walls, ceramics workshops enable young people to discover their talents, and delicious aromas of food surround the catering school where students are training for their future career.

Hark! the herald-angels sing

Pause and remember: a time in the past when you were waiting for physical, emotional or mental healing.

Enjoy today's carol:

Hark! the herald-angels sing
Glory to the new-born King,
Peace on earth and mercy mild,
God and sinners reconciled.
Joyful, all ye nations, rise,
Join the triumph of the skies;
With th'angelic host proclaim,
Christ is born in Bethlehem.
Hark! the herald-angels sing
Glory to the new-born King.

Christ, by highest heaven adored,
Christ, the everlasting Lord,
Late in time behold Him come,
Offspring of a Virgin's womb!
Veiled in flesh the Godhead see!
Hail, the Incarnate Deity!
Pleased as Man with man to dwell,
Jesus, our Emmanuel!
Hark! the herald-angels sing
Glory to the new-born King.

Hail, the Heaven-born Prince of Peace!
Hail, the Sun of Righteousness!
Light and life to all He brings,
Risen with healing in His wings.
Mild, He lays His glory by,
Born that we no more may die,
Born to raise the sons of earth,
Born to give them second birth.
Hark! the herald-angels sing
Glory to the new-born King.

Hark! the herald-angels sing – Lyrics by Charles Wesley, first published in 1739.

Rhama, a woman helped by an Embrace-funded project to regain her sight.

Reflect:

Hark! the herald-angels sing **was originally written by Charles Wesley and went into circulation in 1739, though the melody we now use is different. The lyrics have changed a little in the first verse, but hardly at all in the last, which leads us to a stunning finish as the King of the new kingdom is welcomed to the sound of a soaring descant.**

The singing of *Hark! the herald-angels sing* is usually a gloriously uplifting point in any service. But it is also so familiar that for all the atmospheric joy we feel on hearing it again, we can still end up losing the wonder of the promises we are singing about.

Slow down and read those incredible words again, imagining it is for the first time...

Jesus doesn't leave us to face death, dark and disease alone; He comes to bring His presence and His transformation. He brings light and life; He leaves healing in His wake.

Embrace's partner, the Coptic Evangelical Organisation for Social Services (CEOSS) is inspired by His example. They seek to bring a reflection of His light, life and healing to the lives of those who are struggling. People like Rhama, who lives in Dar-al-Salam, a slum community on the edge of Cairo, in Egypt.

Rhama is 82, and her 17 grandchildren light up her life. But until recently, she was unable to see them due to problems with her eyesight. The treatment she required was not complicated, but in Dar-al-Salam, people with medical problems generally have to muddle through on their own.

There aren't many clinics in the area, and even when there is some healthcare available, many people in the community don't realise they have the right to receive it. So CEOSS' mobile eye clinic goes out looking for people like Rhama – and they found her. Now she can see her grandchildren. She is overjoyed to be healed, and has much more confidence to go to the shops to buy food to cook for her family.

Surely the angels still sing over such wonderful sights...

Pray:

Lord Jesus, help me hear every word sung about you this Christmas as if for the first time. Help me take in the true wonder of you seeking us out to bring light, life and healing. And inspire me to play my part in searching out others in need of transformation too.

Ideas for: meditating on light, life and healing

- Take a few minutes today to light a candle and pray for others living in Dar-el-Salam who don't yet know that CEOSS is aiming to find them and provide a healthcare miracle.

- Write out the third and fourth lines of the last verse of *Hark! the herald-angels sing* and put them up somewhere you will see them often. Each time you do, thank God for Rhama's joy in seeing again, and pray for everyone who still needs to experience light, life and healing across the Middle East today.

Risen with healing

The mobile eye clinics that help patients like Rhama are part of Embrace's mission to provide healthcare to those who don't otherwise have the opportunity to see a doctor. We support general health clinics, too, serving disadvantaged communities in Egypt and the West Bank, and in Gaza we support a hospital that not only deals with the injuries of conflict but also saves lives through early detection of cancer.

See amid the winter's snow

Pause and reflect:

how much Christmas being marked in winter affects how we celebrate it in the UK.

Enjoy today's carol:

See amid the winter's snow,
Born for us on earth below,
See, the Lamb of God appears,
Promised from eternal years:
Hail, thou ever-blessèd morn;
Hail Redemption's happy dawn;
Sing through all Jerusalem,
Christ is born in Bethlehem.

Lo, within a manger lies
He who built the starry skies;
He who, throned in height sublime,
Sits amid the cherubim:
Hail, thou ever-blessèd morn...

Say, ye holy shepherds, say,
What your joyful news today;
Wherefore have ye left your sheep
On the lonely mountains steep?
Hail, thou ever-blessèd morn...

As we watched at dead of night,
Lo, we saw a wondrous light;
Angels singing Peace on earth
Told us of a Saviour's birth:
Hail, thou ever-blessèd morn...

Sacred Infant, all divine,
What a tender love was Thine,
Thus to come from highest bliss
Down to such a world as this:
Hail, thou ever-blessèd morn...

Teach, O teach us, Holy Child,
By Thy face so meek and mild,
Teach us to resemble Thee,
In Thy sweet humility:
Hail, thou ever-blessèd morn...

See amid the winter's snow – Lyrics by Edward Caswall (1814-1878).

Reflect:

See amid the winter's snow is not the first carol we have reflected on which takes inspiration from a winter landscape connected to Europe rather than the Middle East. But a closer look reveals *See amid...* doesn't really set a wintry backdrop for the Nativity at all.

Seeing through the snow is exactly that. We are supposed to be using it to help us imagine beyond it... to an even purer and whiter *'Lamb of God'* appearing through it. It's a visual device to introduce the even bigger story behind the Nativity itself – 'redemption's happy dawn'.

If we can get past this carol's familiarity and freshly see as it suggests we do, it could be a beautiful reminder. It could help us look carefully through all our other traditions so the true meaning of Christmas can again emerge and take centre stage.

There are mixed views on the use of snow in Christmas devotions. It is of course unusual for the setting of the original Christmas story, but not so much for our experience of December in the UK. Today is the shortest day of the year. The nights are drawing in early and there is always the possibility, here at least, that Christmas might be white.

The climate of the Middle East, whilst warmer than our own, is still seasonal; and a quick search of winter in a biblical concordance will find you plenty of references. Winter and spring are also used as metaphors to represent suffering and breakthrough in biblical imagery, as well as in European and American poetic traditions.

The lamb emerging from the snow brings Easter imagery into Christmas, and spring into winter. How appropriate. For this lamb brings the ultimate life and heralds a new season. Winter will turn to spring as He comes – just as C. S. Lewis represented so beautifully in *The Lion, the Witch and the Wardrobe*. Hard, cold hearts will become soft ground, ready to blossom and bear fruit.

In Lebanon today, it is likely to be a few degrees warmer than here, but it will still be cold, especially in the mountains. Communities there are incredibly stretched because the population has nearly doubled with Syrian refugees seeking shelter. But many churches, and the partners Embrace is supporting to help them, are reaching out with food vouchers, blankets, mattresses and other practical gifts.

Warm hearts in Lebanon are reaching out beyond their own limits to help those who are cold. Soft hearts in the UK are reaching out beyond their own comfort to support Embrace's partners.

Surely every time any of us reach out with spring to those experiencing winter, a reflection of that 'gentle lamb... promised from eternal years' is seen more clearly among us again.

Photo credit: Paul Jeffrey

A one-year-old refugee child from Syria, who lives with his parents in a rented 'tent' made from a billboard canvas in Lebanon's Bekaa Valley.

Pray:

Lord Jesus, help me see amid this winter, a clearer picture of you – the gentle Lamb of redemption – emerging into our story to bring new and transforming life. And Lord, help me also perceive this December that there are refugees precious to you – the Lamb of promise – that still need to be seen through this season and brought in from the cold.

Ideas for: helping refugees through the winter

- Go online to look up the temperature today in Lebanon, Syria, Egypt, Jordan and Turkey. Pray for everyone who might be cold, for those providing shelter and warm clothing, and for policymakers debating solutions. Remember too those who have been displaced from Syria, and are currently staying in camps across Europe.

- Refugee families living in treacherous conditions need extra support during the winter. Could you make a donation to Embrace to help with our winter provision for them? Even a small gift could buy a blanket or a pack of rice, making a huge difference to a family struggling to keep warm, dry and fed. To donate, visit **www.embraceme.org** or call **01494 897950**.

On Christmas night all Christians sing

Pause and remember: anyone you know personally who is grieving this Christmas – pray for them now. And if you are experiencing loss yourself, today's tiding is written especially for you.

Enjoy today's carol:

On Christmas night all Christians sing
To hear the news the angels bring,
On Christmas night all Christians sing
To hear the news the angels bring,
News of great joy, news of great mirth,
News of our merciful King's birth.

Then why should we on earth be so sad,
Since our Redeemer made us glad,
Then why should we on earth be so sad,
Since our Redeemer made us glad,
When from our sin He set us free,
All for to gain our liberty.

When sin departs before His grace,
Then life and health come in its place;
When sin departs before His grace,
Then life and health come in its place;
Angels and we with joy may sing,
All for to see the new-born King.

All out of darkness we have light,
Which made the angels sing this night;
All out of darkness we have light,
Which made the angels sing this night:
'Glory to God and peace to men,
Now and for evermore. Amen.'

On Christmas night all Christians sing – Lyrics first published by Luke Wadding in 1684, although it is unclear whether he wrote 'the Sussex Carol' or whether he was recording an earlier composition.

Reflect:

There is no question that today's carol is right to call for joyful songs at the 'news of great joy; news of great mirth'. But the second verse might be hard to sing for some people at the moment – however much they agree that 'the Redeemer made us glad' in overall terms.

Two young women who benefit from a rehabilitation project run by Embrace partner the International Christian Committee in Israel.

Jesus has come. Everything has changed. The kingdom is here... And yet, it is still to come. We cannot – nor should we – avoid acknowledging the truth that there are many reasons why we 'on earth should be so sad'. Collectively, when we consider all that does not match Jesus' standards of peace, love and justice. And individually, whenever any of us face bereavement, loss or injustice in our own lives.

Our Christmas celebrations must make room for some sadness that 2,000 years later, despite history's lessons, man still resist's God's best way; and we are still waiting – as Advent reminds us – for the final coming that will end all loss forever.

Perhaps the third verse of this carol is actually the most helpful in our wrestling. It is conditional – something which needs to be remembered at Christmas if we are to embrace the full truth of the gospel and be sensitive to those of us who might find more comfort in praying some of the bleakest lament psalms than in singing joy-filled carols at present. The lyrics are clear:

'When sin departs before His grace,
Then life and health come in its place.'

Conditionals are good news – they indicate a choice; a chance to partner with Christ's grace to restore life and health to those who have been injured by the sin of unjust treatment.

This life-restoring choice is beautifully exemplified by the staff of Embrace's partner, the International Christian Committee in Israel. They run an education centre in Acre which welcomes girls in crisis and helps rehabilitate them. One of these girls was Doha, a 15-year-old Palestinian girl with Israeli citizenship who was sexually abused and violently attacked at school. She was so frightened she wasn't sure she'd ever be able to enter a classroom again. But thanks to the rehabilitation, space and care she's received at the centre, she is beginning to feel safe, and to be able to imagine a time in the future where she could move forward again.

Pray:

Lord Jesus, help me to still hear through the happy cheer of Christmas carols, the lament or silence of those in a season of grief. Use and strengthen me, and strengthen the education centre in Acre and all Embrace's partners, as we seek to mourn with those who mourn and extend your love and grace so life and health can come again. And Lord Jesus, be yourself my very present help and comfort in every area of loss in my own life too; thank you that you will never leave or forsake me in this life or in eternity.

Ideas for: making space for grief

- Think again about anyone you know who is experiencing loss, including yourself if this is relevant. Is there anything you could do or say – perhaps listening to a favourite piece of music or sharing a meaningful poem – to acknowledge and validate reflection and sorrow amid all the joyful celebration?

- Take a pen and paper and write down the injustices – here and in the Middle East – that you grieve over, and bring them before Christ as an offering alongside your celebration of all He has done. Remember that it is always us catching up with Him in heartbreak for the world, not the other way round. Take some time to share in these sorrows with Him now.

Love came down at Christmas

Pause and decide:

what is your favourite carol of all? What does it bring into focus about the Christmas story for you?

Enjoy today's carol:

Love came down at Christmas,
Love all lovely, love divine;
Love was born at Christmas,
Star and angels gave the sign.

Worship we the Godhead,
Love incarnate, love divine;
Worship we our Jesus:
But wherewith for sacred sign?

Love shall be our token,
Love shall be yours and love be mine,
Love to God and to all men,
Love for plea and gift and sign.

Love came down at Christmas – Lyrics taken from the poem by English poet
Christina Rossetti (1830-1894).

Reflect:

Love came down at Christmas is substantially less famous than *In the bleak mid-winter*, but the lyrics were written by the same poet, Christina Rossetti. They form a simple but beautiful meditation on the most central attribute of the Christmas story – love.

Love divine; love incarnate; love come down.

So many of our favourite carols include the word love, but more in passing. Surprisingly then, *Love came down at Christmas* is unique in focusing so exclusively on it. Its final verse has much in common with how *In the bleak mid-winter* closes though, leading us to a devotional response. There we found ourselves asking 'what can we give?' and concluded our whole hearts were required to thank our King.

Here, we resolve to give back to God in the same language He has given to us – love. It is to be 'our token' – our offering back to Him and the thing we are known for. But this time, two types of love are specified – 'love to God and all men'.

Jesus Himself taught us that love is at the heart of everything. In Luke 10:27, He said: 'You shall love the Lord your God with all your heart, and with all your soul, and with all your strength, and with all your mind; and your neighbour as yourself.' And then He proceeded to expound on who our neighbours are with the story of the Good Samaritan (Luke 10:30-37). This parable is very familiar and yet we always need to hear it again. It is just too easy to walk on by; to be too busy or too full to make time and space for others, even – or perhaps especially – at Christmas.

Samira and her family experienced a desperation few of us can imagine, fleeing their home in Syria and then being evicted from their new apartment in Lebanon because another refugee family could pay the landlord more for it. But one of their neighbours, Hanaan – whose name means compassion – refused to walk by. She spoke to a friend about the family's situation and he let them stay on his land rent free. Then Hanaan and some other Christians provided blankets, mattresses and food vouchers through their local church and the project supported by Embrace.

'Love shall be our token... Love to God and to all men'.

Refugees in Lebanon collecting new mattresses funded by Embrace supporters.

Pray:

Lord Jesus, help me remember this one little word and the huge weight of all it means. L-O-V-E. You are it. You give it. And you call me to be it and give it too. Show me who and how today Lord, because I love you and I long to love all men and women too.

Ideas for: making love your token

- Pray for Samira and all refugees who have experienced hate, fear or rejection. Pray for all Embrace's partners and supporters and for all organisations and individuals reaching out to refugees, that they might minister 'love all lovely, love divine'.

- Write the word 'LOVE' on some gift tags – but instead of attaching them to presents, tie them to ordinary objects you will see and use often over the next few days. Every time you see one, remember why Jesus came to ordinary places and people and how He commanded us to live. Then pray for those who are effectively still waiting by the roadside.

Of the Father's love begotten

Pause and breathe: take a moment to be still and to do nothing. It's Christmas Eve! Peace be with you.

Children build a snowman in the shadow of the Church of the Nativity, Bethlehem.

Photo credit: Mazur/www.catholicnews.org.uk.

Enjoy today's carol:

Of the Father's love begotten,
Ere the worlds began to be,
He is Alpha and Omega,
He the Source, the Ending He
Of the things that are, that have been,
And that future years shall see,
Evermore and evermore.

O that birth for ever blessèd,
When the Virgin full of grace,
By the Holy Ghost conceiving,
Bare the Saviour of our race,
And the Babe the world's Redeemer,
First revealed His sacred face,
Evermore and evermore.

O ye heights of heaven adore Him,
Angel hosts His praises sing,
Powers, dominions, bow before Him,
And extol our God and King.
Let no tongue on earth be silent,
Every voice in concert ring,
Evermore and evermore.

Of the Father's love begotten – Lyrics translated by J M Neale in 1851 from the Latin Corde natus by the Roman poet Aurelius Prudentius.

Reflect:

Of the Father's love begotten sets the Christmas story in its true and magnificent timescale – at the very centre point of human history; and invites us to think of Christ not just as a baby but as the one who is:

'... the Source, the Ending He
Of the things that are, that have been,
And that future years shall see,
Evermore and evermore.'

The Advent of Christmas is drawing to a close. The waiting is almost over. And tomorrow we will arrive at the day we have been anticipating for the last twenty four. Everything we've been preparing for is finally about to start.

Advent has become the busiest season of the year for our whole culture, and the one when people spend the most money. It is also when our churches are most active. And then, just as we've announced again that the Saviour of the world is born... everything goes quiet.

Epiphany (marking the wise men's visit) and Candlemas (celebrating Jesus' presentation at the Temple) are both still to come. But not many people mark them, and even if they do, these celebrations rarely, if ever, carry the same colour or weight as Christmas.

But Jesus' birth is not an ending! It is a beginning; the beginning of a new kingdom and of redemption's story... a story of hope we are still living in, with many more chapters that we must continue helping to write.

This is our penultimate Advent reflection – tomorrow's tiding of comfort and joy is the final in this series of devotions. But the end of this booklet doesn't need to be an ending either. It can also be a beginning...

Today's tiding is the last day we're suggesting ideas for actions, and these ones are a bit different. They're all about looking beyond the big day tomorrow and deciding if you want to carry on the journey of discovery we have begun together this Advent.

Thank you for faithfully joining Embrace this December, singing of comfort and joy all the way.

Together, we've travelled through Advent and across the holy ground of our hearts and the lands of the Middle East, to better prepare our lives for Christ and His kingdom. We are ready for tomorrow. And then...

Pray:

Lord Jesus, here I am, on the eve of celebrating the hinge of history when you – the Source and the Ending of all things – broke into time via Bethlehem, with a brand new beginning for the whole world. Keep me thankful beyond tomorrow and show me how to be part of extending your comfort and joy to many more people across the Middle East, long after my Christmas celebrations are finished for this year.

Ideas for: applying these tidings to the year ahead

• Syrian Christian tradition has typically kept children waiting until New Year's Day for their presents… which are said to be brought by one of the wise men's camels, rather than Father Christmas. Make a note in your diary for 1 January to spend some time thinking back over all we have looked at this Advent, and praying about how to keep journeying with the people of the Middle East in the coming year.

• Keep in touch with more regular opportunities to bring comfort and joy to people across the Middle East in the year ahead; sign up to receive our Re:Action emails at **www.embraceme.org/keep-touch** or call **01494 897950** to talk about other ways you can stay connected.

Away in a manger

Pause and thank God: for sending His precious Son.
Happy Christmas from everyone at Embrace!

Enjoy today's carol:

Away in a manger, no crib for a bed,
The little Lord Jesus laid down His sweet head.
The stars in the bright sky looked down where He lay –
The little Lord Jesus asleep on the hay.

The cattle are lowing, the Baby awakes,
But little Lord Jesus, no crying He makes.
I love Thee, Lord Jesus! Look down from the sky,
And stay by my side until morning is nigh.

Be near me, Lord Jesus; I ask Thee to stay
Close by me for ever, and love me, I pray.
Bless all the dear children in Thy tender care,
And fit us for heaven to live with Thee there.

Away in a manger – Lyrics taken from the carol first published in the 19th century; researchers have yet to confirm the original lyricist.

Reflect:

Lying in a makeshift manger, designed for cattle not kings. Here He is, the Lord of all.

Probably, actually, making quite a lot of crying some of the time. Here He is, the light of the world.

All the traditions; all the carols; all the clutter; all the comfortable, crowded familiarity of Nativity images... Please, God, let them never drown out our wonder.

The God-baby – so precariously and generously given – lies helplessly in straw. For us. And suddenly, centuries of promised redemption have skin. It's real, God's love is being lived out in tiny wrinkles and gurgling cry.

Messiah has come. Because of God's love; to reconcile us in love. And if we let Him, to show us – who so easily forget we are made in His image – how to love like Him.

Today, let's journey together to meet another tiny new baby in Lebanon, alongside the one we already know in Bethlehem. Holding this baby is another set of parents who were far from home, looking for makeshift ways to care for their baby in extreme circumstances.

Here are Pastor Michael and his wife Rita who have welcomed this family in extraordinary, ordinary ways. They refused to be overwhelmed by the scale of the world's brokenness on show in Lebanon, where over 1.5 million Syrian refugees are seeking shelter. Instead they prayed God would use their precarious generosity to help. And so, with support from Embrace, they translated love into baby blankets, nappies, mattresses and warm clothes and gave them to this baby and his proud parents. And this family understood it and they were overwhelmed with comfort and joy.

It's amazing what precarious generosity can do.

Pray:

Lord Jesus,
God-baby lying so vulnerably and starkly in a dangerous world, awaken me with your cries to the love you took such desperate measures to live out in Israel on that very first Christ-with-us day.

Lord Jesus,
precarious and generous example of love translated into action to all who will open their hearts to you, bless everyone who hears your cries echoed by other children and adults in desperate circumstances in the Middle East today. Speed them all the resources they need to help those they long to serve.

Lord Jesus,
risen Lord of all, you have done enough to transform this dangerous world forever. Awaken me to your overwhelming hope and put me to living out your reckless love in precarious generosity. For your sake and till you come again in glory, and no crying is ever made again.

Amen.

Tidings of Comfort and Joy

EMBRACE
the Middle East

Embrace the Middle East
is a Christian charity with
over 160 years' experience
helping people of all
faiths and none to free
themselves from a life of
poverty and injustice.

Together with local
Christian communities
we're bringing lasting
change to the Middle
East through education,
healthcare and community
development projects.

Join us and together we
can bring comfort and joy
to the people of the Middle
East this Christmas.

Get back to the real meaning of Christmas with Embrace. Our Christmas
carol inspired reflections will bring you tidings of comfort and joy from
the Middle East every day of Advent.

So prepare to walk across Holy Land, in your heart and
the Middle East, as we share 25 precious moments of
space with Jesus, and experience His wonder shining
through all the distracting busyness of this season.

Embrace the Middle East
24 London Road West, Amersham, Buckinghamshire HP7 0EZ
01494 897950 • info@embraceme.org • www.embraceme.org
Registered Charity Number: 1076329

ISBN 978-1-9998657-0-2

9 781999 865702 >